A Hat for Pong

By Sascha Goddard

"Today is the best day!"
said Nat.

Nat wants to dress up.

Nat gets a big red hat.

"And I will put that on, too!"

Nat grabs her pet cat, Pong.

Nat puts fat dots on Pong!

Pong gets a little red
hat, too.

Pong is **not** happy!

Nat chats to Pong.

"It will not be for long, Pong!"

Nat pats the mad cat.

Dad and Nat go out
with Pong.

Nat spots lots of kids.

"Nick is a black bat!"
said Nat. "Ying is a rat!"

"That's a lot of chocs!"
said Dad.

"You can have some, Dad,"
said Nat.

"But Pong can not have chocs!" said Nat.

"Put that bag on the mat for Pong," said Dad.

Pong sat in the bag.

He was happy!

CHECKING FOR MEANING

1. Who is dressed up as a black bat? *(Literal)*

2. Where did Pong sit at the end of the book? *(Literal)*

3. Where did Nat get the chocs from? *(Inferential)*

EXTENDING VOCABULARY

grabs	Look at the word *grabs*. What does it mean? What is another word that has a similar meaning to *grabs*?
That's	Look at the word *That's*. Why does it have an apostrophe before the *s*? What two smaller words is *That's* short for?
chocs	What is the word *chocs* short for? What other words can you think of that are short for another word?

MOVING BEYOND THE TEXT

1. What would you dress up as for Halloween? Why?

2. Have you ever had to wear something you were not happy in? What was it?

3. What are some other events that people dress up for?

4. Which character in the book did you like the best? Why?

SPEED SOUNDS

at	an	ap	et	og	ug

ell	ack	ash	ing

PRACTICE WORDS

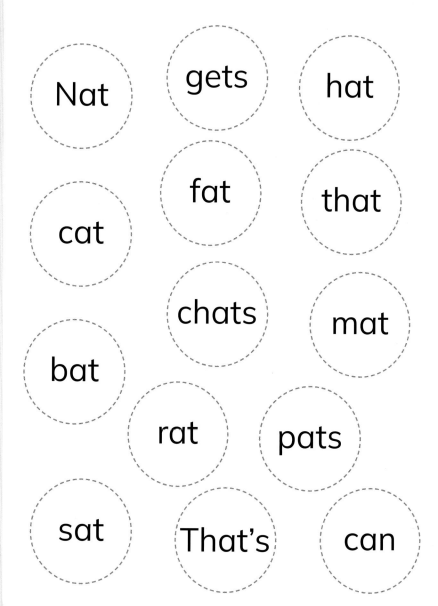

Nat

gets

hat

fat

that

cat

chats

mat

bat

rat

pats

sat

That's

can